BLACK COUNTRY
Jokes & Humour

Doug Parker

roadside

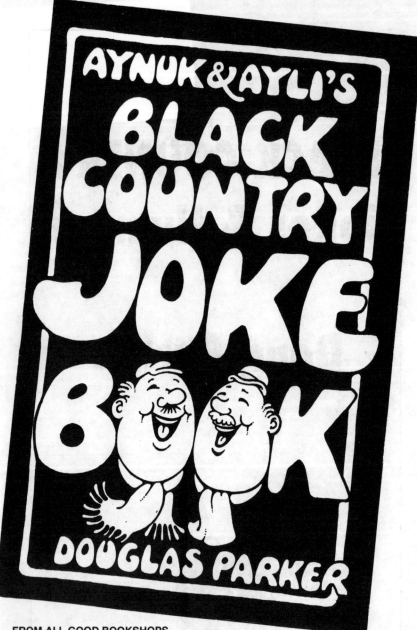

FROM ALL GOOD BOOKSHOPS
OR
DIRECT FROM BROADSIDE AT £1.80 + 60p post/packing

Foreword

I first met Doug Parker in the very early eighties when he appeared at a regular song evening I was involved with at the Rock Hotel, Tettenhall, Wolverhampton. After three or four visits to the weekly 'entertainments' he asked if he could get up and 'do a bit.' I wondered what on earth he would do and reluctantly handed the reins over to him for ten minutes.

Along with the rest of the audience, I was staggered! Doug's chat with the capacity crowd turned out to be a classic, hilarious, humorous observation of life. The ten minutes turned into half an hour and, finally, I was obliged to 'haul' Doug off because we were in danger of breaking the licensing laws.

After that Doug appeared every week to the same wrapt and appreciative reception.

In the years that followed he became a mature and professional trooper. By late eighty one he had joined the famed Black Country Night Out show organised by me and rapidly became a supreme craftsman of comedy and observational humour. During that time he has been the author/co author of five books- 'You must be joking', 'Aynuk and Ayli's Black Country Joke Book,' 'Theodore, a rather curious cat,' 'Theodore, the waterwise cat,' and this new Black Country joke book. In addition he has appeared with the show and as a solo comic in hundreds of concert shows from the Hippodrome in Birmingham to the smallest British Legion club and has also made numerous radio and television broadcasts, both as an entertainer and an actor.

This new book is not just a Black Country joke book. It also explores the world of observational humour and touches on Doug's personal and changing philosophies of life.

If you get the chance to watch Doug's work don't hesitate. He has a rare and engaging talent matched only by his friendly and generous personality. Those who have seen him will already know this!

Jon Raven, August 1991.

Acknowledgments

First published in Great Britain by Broadside in 1991
Copyright © Doug Parker 1991.

ISBN 0 946757 12 7

First impression: Autumn 1991
Copyright: Doug Parker

Studley House,
68 Limes Road,
Tettenhall,
Wolverhampton, WV6 8RB.

OTHER BOOKS BY DOUG PARKER

1. AYNUK AND AYLI'S BLACK COUNTRY JOKE BOOK
2. YOU MUST BE JOKING
3. THEODORE A RATHER CURIOUS CAT
4. THEODORE, THE WATERWISE CAT

BLACK COUNTRY Jokes & Humour 5

Aynuk and Ayli went to the posh convention centre in Birmingham to see a classical concert. Aynuk had never been before and he was watching the conductor for quite a time until eventually he whispered to Ayli,
"Wot meks that mon so angry? They're playin' as fast as they con, ay they?"

Gaffer: "Yo certainly ask high wage for a bloke with no experience,"
Ayli: "Ar but it's harder work when yo doh know what yo'm doing!"

Blackcountry Kids are tough these days, aren't they?
In Quarry Bonk, if you ask, "How are you?"
They say,
  "Who wants to know?"

A little lad was in the Merry Hill Centre standing near an escalator watching the handrail as it moved along.
"What are you up to?" asked the security man.
  "Nothin'" says the little 'un, "I'm just waitin' for me chewin' gum to cum round again."

6

Aynuk and Ayli were sitting by the cut doing a spot of fishing.

Aynuk:

"I bet yo a fiver as I gets a bite afore yo dun."

Ayli:

"Yo'm on, our kid."

Moments later Ayli pulled a giant fish out of the water and, as he was reeling it in, he was so excited he fell into the cut.

"That ay fair," says Aynuk, "If yo'm gonna dive for 'em the bet is off."

Ayli opened his pay packet and he wor 'appy.

"Well ay that someat," he moaned. "They must 'ave gid me a rise 'cos I've got less tek 'ome pay."

Early January
The new year is barely soiled.
There is still hope and expectancy in the air.
Kids are back at school and grateful mothers
attack 'the sales' with a new found spring that
testifies that it seems ages yet until half-term!

7

Aynuk says, "There are times in life when it is wise
   not to be too clever."
He reckons that must mek Ayli a flippin' genius.

Grown ups are stupid
*Do you remember some of the soft things we were
taught as kids?*

We went to Cubs.
*We met in a wooden hut. The first thing they did was
teach us how to light a fire!*

Then there was swimming.
*Remember how they stood us by the side of the baths in
our pyjamas and made us dive into the pool to get a
brick off the bottom? I was only eight but I can
remember thinking at the time, "This is going to be
really useful when I grow up. If ever I'm walking by
the cut at two o' Clock in the morning I shall be able to
dive in and get a brick out!"*

And who can forget Algebra?
$X-Y=Z^2$ *Who cares? And what has it got to do with
the price of sausage? The teacher used to set us
problems like, If A is in the bathroom emptying the bath
faster than C. How much water has B got?*

*It was no good asking me, we'd got a shower in our
house!*

8

Mothers and Kids.

Didn't you just hate it when you were a child and your mother noticed a spec of dirt on your face? She would take out her handkerchief, spit on it and then wipe your face with it. And when she washed your hair in the sink she nearly pushed your head down the plughole.

Mothers knew how to brush hair when we were kids. It felt like they were beating an egg. But mother knew best. That's why she put you to bed when it was light and you were wide awake. Then got you up in the dark when you were tired.

But you knew your mother loved you 'cos she kept hitting you to prove it.

Do you remember getting lost in a big store in town? You would squeal the place down until your mother arrived. She was so pleased to find you she would beat you up!

I hated going shopping with my mother for clothes. Mothers always bought you things to grow into. I've got a pair of khaki shorts at home I still haven't grown into. You could get a whole scout troup into those shorts. I finally had to tell her,

"I'm a man, mother, I'm not going to grow anymore!"

9

Mid January
I wonder how many new year resolutions have
fallen by the wayside?
How many diets have fallen by the fridge?
So often we disappoint ourselves,
Our ideals broken, our good intentions lost.
Such is human frailty.
Like a meringue hammer hitting a brick wall.
Why are we always so surprised?

Aynuk:
   "*Ow cum yo gorra zero on yer school report?*"
Tommy:
   "*That ay a zero. The teacher ran out of stars so 'e
gid me a moon.*"

Aynuk:
   "Why 'av yo gorra knot in yer 'anky?"
Ayli:
   "That's to remind me to post a letter for the
missus."
   "'Av yer posted it?"
Ayli:
   "No, 'er forgot to gi' it me."

10

Somebody once said,
"He was a bold man who first swallowed an oyster."
Aynuk says that the fust to swallow a faggot wor lackin' in courage neither!

Aynuk and Ayli went on a trip to Runnymede 'cos they like to get out now and then. They saw a sign which read,
'Magna Carta signed 1215.'
"Would yo believe it, " said Ayli, looking at his watch, "We've cum all this way and we've missed it!"

Overheard in the Blackcountry,
"Has the next bus gone yet?"

The Buffalos were playing the Masons at golf. One spectator arriving late asked the score.
"I don't know," came the reply,
"It's a secret."

11

You don't know you are born!

I find myself saying,
"What is the world coming to?"
and,
"The kids today, they don't know they are born."
It bothers me because I can remember my parents saying the same things when I was a youth. We called it the generation gap. How they hated the mop-topped Beatles and loathed the Rolling Stones.

"You don't know you are born." I was told.

"In my day we had to get up at 4 o'clock in the morning and do six paper rounds before we went to school. And all that on a bowl of porridge which had to last us 'til we got home at night."

I remember promising myself that I would never utter such rubbish when I was an adult. But I'm seeing things and thinking words I vowed not to repeat.

I get waves of nostalgia. A sudden desire to buy liquorice bootlaces and kick cans down the street. I believe the world is not such a friendly place to live in. I think there is an absence of care. The younger generation would say it's because I'm getting older. But what do they know?

"They don't know they are born."

12

Aynuk, Ayli and 'arry had their own furniture removal business. So they're up and down the stairs at a posh house in Halesowen. Aynuk and 'arry wus strugglin' wi' an old oak wardrobe and they noticed that Ayli wor about.

"Weer yo gon Ayli, we needs yo to 'elp."

"I'm doin the best I con." came the muffled reply, "I'm inside holding the coothangers in place."

The sun is shining,
new buds blink at the stark sunlight.
Then in a moment it is snowing
and the daffodils put on their ballaclava helmets.
It must be April.

The Industry in the Blackcountry is more competitive now.

For every place in the dole queue there are now six applicants.

"How many barrels of beer dun yo sell in a week?"
"About ten," says the landlord.
"Want to sell more?"
"Ar, but 'ow?"
"Yo could try fillin' the glasses."

13

The first threat of spring to the stock exchange.

The early sun cast sharp shadows across the fields
As a promise of spring teased the air and tantalised
the frosty hedgerows.
Mother natures pregnancy once more fascinated an
expectant nation.
Tempted, tentatively from the cocooned comfort of
satisfied armchairs
Witnessing the first cry of crocus and daffodils that
dared peep inquisitively at the inviting light.
"How good to be alive!" I mused, looking at fields
and sheep as though for the first time.
I nudged my accountant friend for affirmation.
He smiled that chilling calculated smile,
handed down from computer to filofax.
His thoughts spilled out in stark observation,
"I bet a restaurant would make a fortune out here!"

Mother nature winced and
carried on with her business.

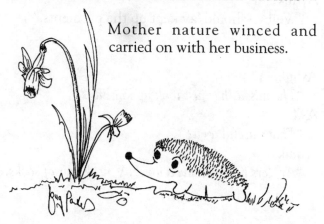

14

When your wife won't speak to you she is trying to tell you something.

Yo know that Aynuk is so saft, 'e thought as an edgehog were a punk rabbit.

'E thought the Charge of the light brigade was an electricity bill.

And he was certain that Joan of Arc was Noah's wife.

'Is missus said as ow she'd like a wood carving of 'im but 'er cor find a piece of wood thick enough.

Ayli:

"The missus says the clocks goo back next week."

Aynuk:

"Well yo should 'av kept up the payments."

Aynuk:

"The missus has just took up knitting."

Ayli:

"That's useful ay it?"

Aynuk:

"Ar, 'ers just med me a lovely V neck pair of socks."

15

Cats.
A cat always sits on your lap just before
you were going to stand up.
You will invariably allow it a few minutes
of your time.
A cat allows *you* the time *it* wants.

*Ayli says that the boss at his last place was the nicest
bloke he'd ever met. He called Ayli into the office and
said, "Ayli, I doh know how we'm gonna manage
without yer but starting from next Monday, we'm
gonna try!"*

Ayli took his missus to the Safari park. As he was
driving through the lion reserve he ignored the
warning signs and wound down the window to take
photographs. His missus was very nervous and
yelled,
  "If yo doh shut that winder straight away, I'm
gerrin' out!"

Aynuk says,
  *"If space scientists are so clever 'ow cum they count
backwards?"*

16

Have you noticed how the council spend three weeks putting a new road down and as soon as they have finished the Gas board come round and dig it up again? There's always a roadworks, no matter where you go. I think there are certain workmen whose job it is to periodically rearrange the potholes.

Aynuk: *"What dun yo think about the Greenhouse effect?"*
Ayli: *"It's probably good for the tomatoes,"*
Aynuk: *"I've bin reading that there's an 'ole in the ozone layer."*
Ayli: *"Cor they put some of that cling film over it?"*
Aynuk: *"Yo doh understand, we've gorra do someat about global warming!"*
Ayli: *"Doh panic, we'll goo an' get a barbecue."*
Aynuk: *"I've 'eard as 'ow we've all gorra goo green."*
Ayli: *"Doh yo worry yerself, the missus says as we two am green enough already."*
Aynuk: *"Dun yo think as we'm environmentally friendly?"*
Ayli: *"We must be, we've never fell out 'ave we?"*

17

"Give us a fiver, Fatso!"

There are lots of slimming classes these days where they 'encourage' you to lose weight by telling you off and insulting you. Then they charge you money for this service. Apparently there is no shortage of takers. A friend of mine said she would like to go to aerobics to try and lose weight. "But," she said, "my backside would look too big in a leotard." Then she went on, "I think I'll go when I'm thinner."

I think we could really help people with a weight problem by making supermarket doors narrow. Then the fat people wouldn't be able to get in! You'd see crowds of overweights outside the window trying to peep at the Jaffa cakes.

Cake shops could help too. In a pub or wine bar if you've had too much to drink, they won't serve you. If a fat person went into a cake shop they should say, "I'm sorry sir, but I think you've had enough!"

People are obsessed by their appearance. We are constantly told we should look one way or another.
"She used to have an hour glass figure but oh how time drags now."
The emphasis is always on youth and people will go to extraordinary lengths to preserve their faces. Some even have facelifts. You can be admiring a dimple in someone's chin little realising it's really their belly button!

18

The Mirror.

The mirror was unkind today
It gave me wrinkles I have not earned.
It's bad enough writing them off to experience
But, in an unkind light the flock of crows feet
claw carelessly across my complexion.
Leaving me to curse the reflection
and seek refuge in dark corners.

When I was young, a moment ago.
My face soft like an unspoilt wench.
Was my mind untainted too?
And, if a face ages with knowledge gained,
Would I not seek to be a fool
and stay young forever?

I usually imagine that lines give me the character of
well worn masculinity.
A man who has seen and knows more than most,
The silent thoughtful type.
One who could proffer advice if asked.
But not to be troubled with mundane, petty
trivialities.

19

When my eyes sparkle and there is a confident spring in my stride,
I tell myself that my body is a vehicle on life's road of experience.
Not in showroom condition, with low mileage and one lady owner,
But reliable on winter evenings.
With the acquired taste of a mature wine that has travelled... rather well.

Then I gaze once more into that infernal mirror with its taunting jibes and stark reports.
And I beg shamelessly that it might show compassion and favour me, more kindly, tomorrow.

20

Aynuk says that Ayli was so lazy that he used to ride his bike over cobblestones to knock the ash off his cigarette.

He went to the doctors once and was told that Alcohol was to blame for all his troubles.

"I wish yo'd tell me missus that," says Ayli, "Er keeps on saying it's my fault."

Aynuks Edukashun

Aynuk says he wasn't very good at history, "'cos everything happened afore I was born."

He says he wasn't very hot at English either, "' cos they day spake much of that in Quarry Bonk!"

*As for maths, he reckons they never needed pocket calculators when he was a kid, "' cos we knew 'ow many pockets **we'd** got!"*

Tipton teacher:

"Tommy, if you had four sweets and I took half of them, what would I have?"

Tommy:

"A broken arm, miss!"

Tomorrow is the first day of the rest of your poll tax.

BEWARE OF THE MANGLE

When the binmen call, the dogs next door go mad. They normally yap a lot, the dogs not the dustbinmen, but when they see the bins being gathered in; it's pandemonium. There's such a clanging from the refuse men. How they make that noise with plastic containers I don't know. The days of metal bins must have seemed unbearable. Dogs, of course, just yap and bark until every canine within a mile radius is committed vocally to the chorus of disapproval.

I ponder that there should be a radio station that broadcasts nothing but silence. .Then, in my quest for peace, I could tune in and, to combat the noise, turn the silence right up, until it drowned everything else out. What bliss that might be – a deafening silence! The neighbours might start banging the walls with shouts of,

"Do you mind, we're trying to have a party in here!" If it caught on no doubt we would get do badders banding together to form a silence abatement society and quiet people would be persecuted for being peaceful in public.

I'm reminded of a lovely story Harry Harrison used to tell about the fellow who complained to his neighbour about the noise his dog made.

"He's gorra bark ay he?" was the response.

"He has not got to bark," said the other firmly. "And if you don't stop him yapping I shall put his tail in the mangle."

"Putting his tail in the mangle woh stop 'im yappin'." said the neighbour. The fellows slow, stern response was, "It will by the time his head comes through!"

22

The worlds unluckiest hedgehog successfully negotiated six lanes of the motorway and was halfway up the embankment when he was run over by a lawnmower.

Aynuk: " I was wondering what to buy the missus for her birthday."
Ayli: "Why doh yo buy 'er a book?"
Aynuk: "That ay no good, 'ers already gorra book."
Ayli: "Sorry mate I wor thinkin'"

Aynuk and Ayli were on holiday together and they stayed at a posh hotel, cruet on the table and everything. The first thing they did was ask what time the food was served.
The desk clerk said,
    "Breakfast is from 7 to 11, lunch is 11.30 to 3, tea is from 4 to 6 and dinner is from 6.30 to 10."
Ayli:
    "That ay no good to us, we woh 'ave time to goo out."

Aynuk says Ayli is so saft he thought a piece of sandpaper was a map of the desert!

23

Pigeons.

Why don't pigeons buy their own sandwiches?
You will notice that wherever people sit to
meditate or snatch a moment or two in
conversation with a friend; there is a pigeon.
When it's a popular lunchtime spot he's there,
strutting up and down, very often with his entire
family. Backwards and forwards they go, pacing
about like expectant fathers at a maternity hospital
waiting for you to deliver. They are not fussy these
pigeons, they'll eat anything. Just get your grub out
and be quick about it..They've got no respect.
I'm sick of hearing them say, "Look at the fool,
Look at the fool," before gobbling up the crumbs
from my lunch.
I reckon anyone who could talk to these birds,
maybe pidgin English, could clean up.
They should open a sandwich shop for pigeons and
make the blighters buy their own.

24

26th. April.

The days are longer now and the air already anticipates the warmth of May.

Perhaps the most splendid time of the year as spring blends with summer in a mercurial marriage of colour and promise.

There is something a little special abroad that teases the most doubting of minds.

Nature shews forth her young again and begs approval.

Then with a nod of blossom on a breeze blown bough,

Courts our attention and demands our heartfelt praise.

Ayli:
"*Dun yo know where me new tie is?*"
Ayli's missus:
"*Yo'm wearin' it yer fool.*"
Ayli:
"*It's a good job yo told me else I'd a gone without it.*"

Hear about the chap who started a microchip business? He was so successful he's looking for smaller premises.

When Humpty Dumpty visits your restaurant you do not recommend the scrambled egg!

25

The Learning Process.

It's a strange thing, this learning process.
The need to be more sensitive,
more aware,
more responsive.
The desire to give of oneself.
To grow,
and to nurture that growing.
To partake of knowledge and to savour life.
All these things give pain.
A finely tuned machine gives more
problems than a simple plough,
Yet may travel no further down the field
without the masters close attention.
But should we not demand of ourselves that
sensitivity?
Until we can perceive a lark three meadows away
And enjoy the beauty of its call,
whilst mourning the loss of its young.
For its song does not become less sweet because of
its sorrow
And its courage demands our applause.
Even so,
because it's a strange thing, this learning process
Pity the man who hears the lark three meadows
away
Yet notices not the sparrow in his own back yard.

26

Ayli: "My brothers cum fer the weekend, Aynuk,
   yo'll 'ave to meet him."
Aynuk: "What's he like?"
Ayli: "Either a pint of mild or a drop of stout."

*Aynuk and Ayli went for a skiing holiday in Scotland.
On the first day they were trekking up the mountains
when along comes a chap on a sledge.*
   Aynuk: "Con yo tell us where the ski slopes bin?"
   Stranger: "It's no good asking me I'm a tobagganist."
   *Aynuk: "In that case, con I 'av twenty Woodbines
and a box of matches?"*

Aynuk: "Ow cum yo've stopped singin' in the
   church choir?"
Ayli: "well I day goo one Sunday and somebody
   asked if the organ 'ad bin mended."

*If they played piped music on buses would it be 'the
refrain from spitting'?*

27

"Listen carefully," said a woman to her friend.
"I can only tell you this once because I promised never to repeat a word of it."

The old days.
Aynuk says that he can remember the old days when he had a tin bath in front of the fire.
His one shoulder was red raw from the heat of the flames. His other was blue from the draught coming under the door.
His grandfather was so fat that when he wanted to take a bath they had to grease the sides to get him in.
Aynuk says they had no jacuzzis in them days. The nearest you got to that was with a spoonful of liver salts in the bathtub.
Happy days!
Ayli says he remembers when they had a po under the bed. They used to say,
"Yo knew it was full when your thumb went warm!"

Ayli says as ow he's bin breeding birds and he's crossed a homing pigeon with a woodpecker.
He's gorra bird that not only delivers messages.....it knocks on the door fust!
Aynuk doh believe 'im neither.

28

Proper food.

It's hard to know what to eat these days.
Everything is bad for you. It wasn't long ago that
they were telling us to 'Drink a pinta milka day.'
Now everyone is frightened of cholesterol so it's
suddenly better to drink water. Not from the tap
mind, you can't trust that stuff, but spring water
fresh from the source and guaranteed to be pure.

But is it? I'm not so sure, not with all that fallout
from Russia. It seems like only yesterday that we
felt confident about the lambs grazing in the North
of England and Scotland. Now they glow in the
dark! Then there's the food poisoning to worry
about. Botulism and Salmonella sound like a
couple of resorts on the continent but they've
taken on a real meaning just lately. It wasn't so
long ago we were invited to 'Go to work on an egg.'
If you eat an egg now you might not be fit enough
to go to work! When we were kids we used to take
a bottle of water straight from the tap in an old
Tizer bottle. Then we'd pass it round, taking it in
turns to take a swig. We survived. My grandfather
never knew about 'proper food'. He thought High
Fibre was a runner in the three o' clock at
Sandown. His diet consisted of lots of bread and
dripping and Belly draft pork. Sometimes, for a
change, he would have a couple of pigs feet. He
would say, "Get this down yer, it will stick to yer
ribs!' He was in his nineties when he died. Mind
you he did have very sticky ribs.

29

Aynuk and Ayli went out night clubbin' 'cos they wanted to walk on the wild side. The first club they arrived at wouldn't let them in 'cos they weren't wearing ties. Undaunted they went back to the car and Ayli took out a set of jump leads. Splitting them in two they tied them round their necks giving Aynuk a red tie and Ayli a black one. Then our heroes went back to the club.

Ayli: "We've got ties on now, con we cum in?"

"Alright," says the doorman, looking at the jump leads, "But don't start anything."

When they got inside they went straight up to the bar, 'cos they doh muck about these two. Aynuk, not wishing to pay fancy club prices for their favourite brew, decided to start with a soft drink.
Aynuk:
"Two glasses of orange, please."
Waiter: (after a pause.)
"Still orange?"
Aynuk:
"Ar, we ay changed our minds yet."

Cats.
The cat who has refused affection all day will knead you with its paws at 3 o' clock in the morning.
A cat expands in direct proportion to the space left on the bed.

30

June
June already....time gallops ever onwards. Here I am
enjoying the warmth of the sun and in the blink of
an eye someone will be saying, "Are you ready for
Christmas?" Sends a chill down a mans back. I stare
hard at the Rhododendron bush so that it is
engraved on my mind. I tried the same trick with
the Laburnum, trying desperately to freeze that
moment in time, and already it is lost until Winter
has once more taken its toll. Time is not a great
friend of mine. He cares not and marches on
undaunted. Like a thief he steals my magic
moments. Yet he lies to me in those troubled times
when he drags his heels contemptuously.
June already......and another petal falls from the
Rhododendron.

A flock of Geese with pointed beaks was flying over
Tipton..'cos they felt daring. Another goose from
another flock noticed that one of the birds had got a flat
beak and asked, "How come you've got a flat beak and
all your mates have got pointed beaks?"
"Well" said the flat beaked goose, " I con fly as fast as
them....but I cor stop as fast."

31

Children's Television.
Kids today watch more television than ever.
Yet have you seen the average children's T. V.
presenter? The Woodentops would have refused to
work with most of them. The 'new crowd' prance
about in the most inane fashion and credit their
audience with the mental capacity of a clothes peg.
Mr. Pastry would not have been amused.

Aynuk says he's just had a double up on the horses....
two non runners.

Aynuk reckons he's a self made man.
  "But." says Ayli, "He never was any good at
meckin' things."

Foreman reprimanding Aynuk:
  "After the firms party yesterday you were spotted
pushing a wheelbarrow round the Savacentre car park
at two o' clock in the morning. Don't you think you
were letting the company down?"
Aynuk: "I cor say it crossed me mind really 'cos yo was
the one in the barrer!"

32

Bills.

There's always a bill to pay. No matter how up to date you are there's always a new bill waiting to come through the door. Even if you never buy anything you get bills.

Take the poll tax. (I wish somebody would.) You are being charged just for being alive. Just for existing.

Let's face it, you are always in debt until you die. Then they send you a bill for your funeral. And if you don't leave enough money to cover it everyone will talk about you. Funerals cost a fortune so if you can't afford to live, you certainly can't afford to die.

If you are poor you might want to die but you've got to hang on until you can afford it. And while you're saving up for it someone sends you another bill and the shock kills you!

You can always tell the posh people in the Black Country.

They are the one's who get a blue electricity bill which they ignore. Some weeks later they get the red reminder. Seven days later they pay the blue bill. What style!

33

It is said that tact will take a person further than cleverness.

Aynuk reckons that's why Blackcountry folk doh travel very far.

Aynuk: "The chap next door has bought a Jacuzzi."
Ayli: "I day know 'e could ride a motorbike."

Aynuk got himself fixed up as a Butler in one of them posh houses at Pedmore. Since he was new to the job his boss kept a close eye on him and watched while he answered the telephone. All the head of the house heard Aynuk say was,

"Ar it is." then put the phone down. This happened three times before the boss, being more than a bit curious, asked Aynuk to explain the conversation.

"Well," said the Blackcountryman, "I picked up the phone and a voice says, 'Long distance from Edinburgh' so I says, 'Ar it is,' then I put the phone down."

Ayli: "Wot dun yo think of this police dog I bought?"
Aynuk: "He doh look much like a police dog to me."
Ayli: "Well the bloke wot sold 'im to me said 'e was in the secret service."

34

The car boot sale.

Like pigeons at the rubbish dump squabbling with the seagulls over scraps–they were waiting. As soon as our car pulled up they crowded in on us, jostling each other for position, anxious to gain a point of advantage. We were not pop stars or some important dignitary paying a visit. Our mission was much more humble. *We* were car booters.

Here we were, on a car park, the early morning sun still with sleep in its eyes; being subjected to the sort of harassment that might accompany a Red Cross visit to the Third World. Had we opened the windows the scavengers would have been inside the car, such was their desire to get at our 'booty'.

"Give me five minutes to set up." I cried, vainly trying to ease the claustrophobia that surrounded me. Hands started to ferret into unpacked cardboard boxes as I wrestled them off the back seat. My jumble was being assaulted before it had had the opportunity to display itself.

"Give me five minutes to set up!" I repeated firmly to ignoring ears.

"How much for this?" said a tightly permed lady holding up a pot.

"Er, a pound?" I ventured, tentatively.

"I'll give you 50p," she countered, pouncing on my hesitancy.

I agreed as she moved off with the flock to pick the spoils from a newly arrived Volkswagen.

35

Taking advantage of this brief diversion my wife won a best of three falls with the trestle table and started to display our oddments whilst I glanced round at our companion traders who were setting up with equal relish. The range of goods on offer was astounding. This was clearly the place to be if you wanted flared trousers or a coffee mug with Kevin Keegan's face on it. No more wondering where those pullovers, bought at Christmas by a distant colourblind Aunt, had gone. They were all here, accompanied by the 'Best of Dicky Valentine' and a hardly used Vick inhaler.

It soon became clear that at a car boot sale the public will buy anything if the price is right. It is also true that you could have the Crown Jewels on offer at a fiver and someone would try to knock you down to a quid. This is not the arena for the sophisticated marketing mind but if it costs less than a pound they just might bite your hand off.....and probably most of your arm. I had taken an old radio, thinking that the parts might be useful to an enthusiast and felt my decision was vindicated when a fellow in a pigeon fanciers scarf enquired the price.

"Twenty pence." I suggested, confidently.

"Does it work?" he quizzed.

I wanted to tell him that for 20p he could hardly expect to pick up the flying doctor but he seemed content to take a chance and will probably end up using it as a door stop in his pigeon loft.

36

My wife had made some rather pleasing padded coathangers and had trimmed them with lace.

"How much?" enquired a female bargain hunter, eyeing them inquisitively.

"Fifty pence." said Mrs. P.

"Each?" she asked.

"No, we give you half a dozen and throw in a Laura Ashley frock," my mind responded sarcastically but I bit my tongue as my wife made the sale and the female bargain hunter scurried off into the crowd. I hoped she'd meet and marry the man who bought the radio. They had so much in common.

I turned the tables on one lady who spent five minutes fingering a small dish. After the most critical inspection, worthy of an item on the 'Antiques Roadshow' she asked the price. "Whatever you feel it's worth." I replied, mentally congratulating myself on my wit. She was completely thrown. "Oh, I don't know," was the flummoxed response, "It's *your* dish!"

And it was. She disappeared leaving it on the table. My wife clearly felt my selling technique was becoming more questionable by the minute and suggested I get the sandwiches out of the car.

The boot sale is a barterers paradise where people will tut quite puckishly if the price doesn't please them. If you offer something at ten pence which is clearly worth ten times that amount the punter will unashamedly offer you 5p and be surprised if you refuse.

The advantage of going as a pair is that you can take it in turns to nip off and look for a bargain on another stall. Then there is the immense pleasure at the end of the morning when tired trestles have been folded away and you wonder why you are taking home more items than you came with.

In years to come people may look back with affection at the custom that is called the car boot sale. It may become part of our folklore.

What a wonderful tradition we are creating where week after week, on car parks across the country, people are gathering together to exchange junk competitively. It's got so much more to offer than Morris dancing, don't you think?

38

Ayli: "I doh think the missus thinks much of me."
Aynuk:"Wot meks yer say that?"
Ayli: "Well, she said she only married me 'cos 'ers afraid of burglars."
Aynuk: "Ers got an 'ard tongue your missus."
Ayli: "I got me own back the other night. 'Er 'eard a noise downstairs and asked me to goo and 'ave a look."
Aynuk: "Wot did yo say?"
Ayli: "I told 'er to goo 'cos 'ers more frightening than me. 'Er ay arf suck 'er gums. Then 'er said, 'When I married yo I thought yo was brave.'
I said, "So did all my mates!"

Frozen assets.
Have you ever looked at an object in the fridge and thought,
"I don't know what it is but it's growing hairs."
Years ago people used to eat everything up or throw it away. Remember the hard cheese we used for toasting?
Then someone invented cling film so that anything we don't use can be covered and put in the fridge.
Then three weeks later you can take it out and throw it away.
My grandmother used to save drops of fat in cups and store them in the pantry. Her Blackcountry philosophy was 'waste not, want not.'
They didn't have fridges years ago but they never ran out of fat.

39

Teacher: "If you found a five pound note in every pocket of your jacket, what would you have?"

Tommy: "Somebody else's coot!"

Teacher: "Tell me one of the products of the West Indies."

Tommy: "I doh know, miss."

Teacher: "You must know where sugar comes from?"

Tommy: "Either Tesco's or the Savacentre."

Teacher: "Where's the English Channel?"

Tommy: "Is it one button down from BBC 1?"

Progress.
Years ago when life was simple,
folk had horse drawn carriages and choked from
the smog caused by chimney smoke.
Then we became environmentally friendly
and introduced smokeless fuels.
So now we have clean air which we pollute
with the motor car.

Ayli was so saft at school that when he was copying off the kid next to him and the kid put, "Don't know."

Ayli put, "Neither do I."

40

Getting Shirty.

Hands up who remembers Bri Nylon shirts. They drip dried and never needed ironing. They also stuck to your back in warm weather and, if you touched anything while standing on a thick carpet, 3,000 volts went up your arm. I can never understand why they sell shirts in collar sizes. Some men have short arms and big chests while others are the opposite with their knuckles almost dragging on the floor. Yet it's your collar size that determines the size of the shirt you get. When a woman goes to buy a blouse the assistant doesn't ask, "And what is the size of madams neck?" You wouldn't go into a shoe shop and expect them to ask you questions about your kneecaps. So why this obsession with collar sizes? And while we're at it, why do they need all those pins when they pack a shirt? By the time you've finished unwrapping you've got enough to specialise in acupuncture. Then a stray pin will invariably stab you in the throat when you try it on.

We are European now, even in the Blackcountry, and we are expected to conform. Goodness knows what Aynuk and Ayli will mek of it. I'm reminded of the story about the fellow who went into a shoe shop and asked to try on a pair of black shoes, size nine. "We doh do 'em now." said the assistant

"Pardon?"

"We'm metric now, ay we."

"So what is it now?"

"It's size 43 now."

So the fellow tried on a size 43 but they pinched his feet.

"These are too tight." he said.

"Oh," said the assistant,

"Yo probably need a nine and a half!"

41

September slips sadly away
Swiftly the chill winds bite
October forces hard against the door
And Winter fingers touch the window pane.

Aynuks missus:
  *"Yoh lied to me afore we was married 'cos yoh told
me yoh was well off."*
Aynuk:
  *"I **was** only I day realise it at the time."*

I see they've got a new kind of street
entertainment in the Blackcountry now
....it's called mugging!
These neighbourhood watch schemes are good.
The neighbours watch your house,
then while you're out they nip in and
pinch the video!
In the Olympic games a chap got a gold medal for
doing 10,000 metres. In the paper last week a bloke
in Lye got six months for doing three meters!

*Aynuk says his wife is so ugly she doesn't use a dressing
table - she's got a workmate!*

42

Dolly Allen.

In 1990 she said "Ello me luvvers" for the last time but many will recall her distinctive style. Her delivery was unique. Dry, flat tones uttered with that deadpan expression. The audience loved her. She was known as the "Queen of Blackcountry comedy" and with her passing we witnessed the end of an era.

At her best talking about her workshy husband who had been on the labour so long he'd worn four pairs of pumps out.

"He went after the job and I could tell he'd got it as soon as 'e cum in. He day look a bit 'appy."

He asked the gaffer, "How much dun yo pay 'ere?"
The gaffer says, "I pay a mon wot 'e is worth."
He says, "That ay no good to me, I got more than that at the last place!"

To give him some encouragement to go to work she got up early and called up the stairs, "Wot yo want fer your breakfast?"
'E says, "An 'ot pie and call me when it's cold!"
She says, "E day want to goo."
He says, "It's foggy, yo cor see the rooftops."
She says, "Yoh doh goo that road!"

43

Her jokes typified Blackcountry thinking
and embodied the best of its humour.

I thought, I'll gerrim summat for 'is tay. So I went
to the fishap. I says, "I'll have a pair of kippers
please."
The bloke says, "I'm sorry missus I ay got a pair of
kippers in the place."
I said, "Two odduns will do."

She took a pair of shoes to the cobblers and, when
told that it cost 15 shillings to sole or ten shillings
to heel, simply replied,
"Yo con 'eel these all the way up."

Everything she said was so matter of fact.

She talked about the fellow who had two fingers in
bandages after he'd trapped them in a
machine at work. He only injured one
at fust but they day believe 'ow he'd
dun it so he had to show them!

It made sense to Dolly.
It made sense to
her audience.
She will be
greatly missed.

"GOODBYE ME LUVVERS!"

44

Are you receiving me?

I've noticed as I've travelled abroad, even as far as Pensnett, television aerials on the rooftops tend to point the same way, normally in the direction of the transmitter. Except that there is usually *one* pointing in a different direction to all the others and I can't help thinking, "What's he watching?" Has he found a channel the rest of us don't know about? We're a nation obsessed by television, as the number of satellite dishes, clinging to the side of houses like giant frisbees, will verify. There are dozens of stations available now and, thanks to cable, dozens more to come. People will eventually have several videos so that they can watch the stuff they recorded yesterday, today, while recording today the stuff they will watch tomorrow. Another machine will record the programmes we haven't got time to watch but feel we should keep in case it rains at Wimbledon again. A video, up the corner, will be taping anything we might miss while we're out buying more blank tapes and picking up the latest blockbuster from the hire shop. Eventually we will all have to stay at home full time to catch up with the items we are missing and this will mean that nobody will work which will mean that we will no longer need programmes like Central Jobfinder which will be replaced by a video, the soundtrack of which will be available on cassette or compact disc from a stockist near you. Phew!

Cats.
A cat always gives *you* as much affection as *it* needs.

Ayli:
   "I'm doing a fust aid course at werk and I've gorra tek a test tomorra. Ask us a question from this book, will yer?"
Aynuk:
   "If someone was bleeding heavily from a head wound what would you do?"
Ayli: (after much thought)
   "Apply a tourniquet to his neck?"

October
Today is Autumn,
Tomorrow is Winter,
And cold hearts thrive when days are short.
So far they stretch beyond horizons
Where new year promise may come to nought.
But still the hope of springtime chances
Will court the heart as days pass through.
A chill bleak wind may break the spirit
The fresh sap begs me start anew.

46

Bonfire night

Bonfire nights were eagerly awaited when I was a kid. I remember collecting fireworks for weeks before, keeping them in a shoebox until the 'big night'. Every now and then we'd get them out to look at them and count how many we'd got. Sparklers were counted individually because that way you felt as if you had more.

It always managed to rain on November 5th, and it seemed an eternity before your dad came home from work. Then you were ready for the action. After much tutting from father, who was struggling to encourage damp wood to burst forth, the bonfire was lit.

Everyone cheered and it promptly went out again. Several false starts later and the night sky was aglow. There was always a great anticipation as we warmed ourselves. The sound of the fire, was our taster before the main event.

"Fireworks, dad, Fireworks!" was the chorus from a family audience growing restless for their pyrotechnic pleasure. Were they worth waiting for? Grandma always went indoors after the first jumping jack. Catherine Wheels never wanted to go round and invariably stuck and fizzled on the line prop. Then one of the Roman Candles would fall over and burn a hole in the lawn. The sparklers took ages to light. You needed about six boxes of matches for each one or better still a portable bunsen burner.

47

We had never heard of lasers in those far off days but we made our own by waving the sparklers round and round in the air leaving a line in the darkness. Some did figures of eight. You could spell your name if you were quick and called Bob. If you were a Geoffrey or a Henrietta you had no chance.

Do you remember waiting all night for the 'taters' to cook and then getting butter all over your mittens? Then it was a cup of cocoa and off to bed with young eyes peeping out of the bedroom window eagerly searching the skyline for signs of activity elsewhere. Next day we all walked round the streets looking for rocket sticks and sniffing the sulphur hanging in the air.

It was a great night, wasn't it?

These days the government are starting to discourage people from having their own fireworks because they can be dangerous. So they've filled the country with cruise missiles instead!

Two sparrows sat on a rooftop on bonfire night. Suddenly a rocket fizzed past into the night sky.

"Gee," said one, "I wish I could fly that fast."

"Yo would," said the other, "If *your* bum was on fire!"

48

Our two chums were working on the building site.
Aynuk swung his sledgehammer and smacked Ayli
a right corker on the side of his head.
"Wot yo up to?" shouted Ayli, (loosely translated)
"Yo'm mekkin' me bite me lip!"

*Aynuk, who had drunk too much the night before woke
up in Russells Hall hospital bandaged from head to foot.*
*"Thank goodness yo've cum round." said Ayli, who
was sitting by the bed sucking a grape.*
"What happened?" asked Aynuk
*"Well," said Ayli, "I ay sid nothin' like it afore.
When we cum out of the pub yo climbed to the top of
the Merry Hill centre and said yo was gonna fly round
Brierley Hill."*
*"I thought yo was my mate," said Aynuk, "Why day
yo stop me?"*
*"Because," said Ayli, "Last night I thought yo could
do it."*

A little advice from Ayli who has no love of car
engines or their complexities.
"Never lift a bonnet unless it's got a pretty face
underneath."

49

Age Concern

There's a lot of talk about the age gap and the supposed chasm between different generations. The more I think about it, however, the more young people and oldsters have in common. Consider:- When you are young if you get a pain they say, "Don't worry, it's a growing pain." When you are older and you feel a twinge it's, "Don't worry, it's your age." When you are young and you want to make a point they won't listen to you simply because you are only a kid. And because you are young you won't listen to anybody yourself. When you are old they won't listen to you because they think your marbles have gone. "It's his mind, it wanders!" And you try to listen to them but you can't 'cos your going deaf. When you are young you've got an opinion on everything but really you know nothing. When you get into your thirties you realise how little you know so you say nothing. You keep your mouth shut. By the time you are forty you are already being told that you're stuck in your ways. The kids think you are past it. You are an embarrassment to your family. By the time you are fifty they think, "Are you still here?" Anything after that and you'd better play bowls and keep quiet if you know what's good for you. When you reach your eighties you've seen life and have got a good story to tell. Trouble is you can't remember what it was and besides you'd rather have a mug of cocoa and an early night.

50

Our Molineux Pilgrimage.

When I was a child and saw for the first time the famous gold and black,
I greeted each match day with an excited optimism.
"They are a great team, aren't they, Dad?"
I said, pressing my woolly hat proudly into place.
"They used to be!" said father recalling the floodlit fifties and muttering things like,
"Not fit to lace Billy Wrights boots this lot."
But we went Father and I, my hand in his,
Our Molineux Pilgrimage.

When I was a man I put away childish things.
Well, my woolly hat had shrunk from too many rainy Saturdays in the Cowshed.
The team had changed but the colours remained the same.
"They're not a bad team, are they, son?" my father said.
While I was muttering something about Peter Knowles and his bootlaces.
But we went Father and I, shoulder to shoulder,
Our Molineux Pilgrimage.

When we started winning again, the famous gold and black
He greeted each match day with cheerful expectancy.
"They're a good team, aren't they, son?" said father with a twinkle in his eye.
"They could go right back to the top!"
"They're not so bad," I countered, mentally considering
the gulf between our team and the league's elite;
probably several grades of bootlaces apart.
But we went Father and I, my arm around his shoulder
Our Molineux Pilgrimage.

Dedicated to the memory of my father,
Edgar Thomas Parker.

51

They don't write them like they used to.
There was a lovely song written a few years
ago which went,
If I were a carpenter
And you were a lady
Would you marry me anyway?
Would you have my baby?

If that were written today it would probably go,
If I were a welder
And you worked on Woolworth's pick 'n' mix
Would you be my common law wife?
Would you have my lovechild?

*Aynuk says he's just bought a smashing motor. "It's
only 'ad two owners. One called Godfrey Davis and a
Dutch chap called Hertz Van Hire."*

Holiday tip.
When away from home don't forget to take your
wife into Marks and Spencer or C and A to stop
her getting withdrawal symptoms.

*Aynuk watches so much television that if it wasn't for
Emmerdale Farm he wouldn't get any fresh air at all.*
*He even misses his walk down the garden now that
they've got an inside toilet.*

52

Mrs Alcocks Slide

I remember as a child the great thrill we had when the cold weather drew in and the pavements started to glisten with ice. I don't know who started the slides – it was probably the first pair of juvenile feet that saw light of day. For a young pair of shoes could never walk on icy floors – they had to pick up speed and slide. We did not think too much about older people it has to be admitted. Pavements made great slides for us kids, that's all we knew, irrespective of the problems faced by the stiffer, uncertain legs that had to follow. Indeed we viewed quite dimly the interference of Mrs. Alcock who would twitch lace curtains in annoyance then appear moments later with a bucket of ash. In seconds a lovingly prepared slide was reduced to a cinder track and she would stalk off, her stockings round her knees, clucking in an irritated fashion.

We didn't like Mrs. Alcock. She had a low tolerance to kids in any climate.

Even in the warmth of summer if a stray ball dared have the temerity to wander into her garden it was a short straw job to decide who would retrieve it. Her catchphrase was, "Go and play up your own end!" and most of the time we did. But there was a grand slope, an irresistible slope in winter, just outside her house. It begged us to make a slide. And children can seldom resist a beggar.

53

Aynuk:

"When the mon cum to empty the meter he asked me why there was a lot of foreign coins in it."

Ayli:

"Wot did yo say?"

Aynuk:

"I told 'im it wor my fault as the missus did a lot of continental cooking."

Strange world.
Ask people to stand in a confined space with a missile flying around at a 100 m.p.h and they would tell you to forget it. Call it squash and they all want to play.

Aynuk and Ayli were at the multi screen cinema at Merry Hill. Aynuk went to get some popcorn while Ayli went to pay for their seats. When he rejoined his friend he noticed that Ayli had bought extra tickets.

"Why have you bought so many tickets?" asked Aynuk.

"Well," said Ayli, "Last time, the lady over there tore mine up."

He who laughs last is probably as thick as Aynuk and Ayli.

54

Driving me crazy.

How come lorry drivers, on the motorway, always drive right up your tail bumper? I'm convinced they would climb onto your back seat if they could. And why do coach drivers always leave their engines running when they are waiting for their passengers? The motorists that really puzzle me are those who think they can park wherever they like as long as they put their hazard lights on. You've all seen them on double yellow lines or some other restricted spot, very often half on the pavement and half off. Then they will stroll out of the off license/video shop and smile benignly at the obstructed traffic with an expression that says, "It's alright pal, I've got my hazard lights on." I believe these motorists would park in the middle of Woolworths if they could get their car past the cash till. They are probably the same people who empty their car ashtrays onto car parks or into the gutter. While they've got their hazards lights on, of course!

Aynuk:
"I doh know why but I con always win at cards but I doh no good on the 'osses."
Ayli:
"That's 'cos they doh let yer shuffle the 'osses."

Aynuk:
"Ow cum yo've gorra big black smudge on yer face, our kid?"
Ayli:
"It's 'cos the missus has gone to stay with her sister for a month and when I took her to the station I kissed her goodbye."
Aynuk:
"But 'ow cum yo've gorra smudge?"
Ayli:
"Well as soon as I'd put her on the train I went and kissed the engine!"

Aynuk says his missus has spent the last twenty years changing his habits and now complains that he's not the man she married!

What have buses and Jehovah's Witnesses got in common?
Answer:−
They usually arrive in pairs.

56

I don't want to upset anyone in Telford but...

I was talking to someone about Telford, the town the planners made. Where getting off the ringroad is an artform in itself. It appears to be totally lacking in warmth. There is something antiseptic about its presence. A legoland of buildings and roads and then more roads which inevitably lead to a garage to refuel so that you can get out on the road again. I've nothing against Telford, it just does not seem to have much going for it.

Now Wolverhampton on the other hand has been the butt of many jokes. It's easy to poke fun at its cosmopolitan working class society but it's an old established town of character. A town built for the people who lived there. It has wrinkles which show its age, but it also has a heart which pumps as strongly in the 1990s as it did at the turn of the century. In recent times, in Wolverhampton, they built the ring road. It's so close to the town it threatens to strangle the old place. And Prince Consort on his horse appears to be moving faster than the traffic that ventures into the web of one way systems.

The Telford ring road, by comparison, is like some sprawling umbilical cord which presumably disappears up its own navel. I'm sure the people of the town are the same assorted selection as in any area but it is extremely difficult to find anyone who actually admits to being a local. 'Telfordites' are thin on the ground. They probably all live in a dormobile that continually cruises the ring road laughing at outsiders vainly trying to get in. Telford is twinned with the Bermuda Triangle. You hear of people going there but you never see them again.

57

I've got a sneaky suspicion that Lord Lucan is the mayor and that Shergar nibbles grass in a field somewhere near an old air craft once owned by Glenn Miller.
Be honest, you've never seen a car sticker boasting,
'I've been to Telford'
have you?
'I've been on Telford ring road and come home again'
is much more appropriate.

Then there's Redditch...........

Redditch is the town that invented the sign 'All other districts' Whoever lives in all other districts should have no difficulty getting home.
Getting anywhere else in Redditch is something of a challenge but ' All other districts' is a doddle..
The road system that surrounds the town is made up of about 68 runways left over from the now completed Birmingham International airport.
They go on forever and they all direct you to 'All other districts'
One day someone may have the bright idea of linking Redditch to the Telford ring road system.
It could make negotiating Spaghetti Junction a non event.

58

Aynuk and Ayli were playing Bingo down at the Social.
"64"
"Look Ayli yo've got that 'un."
"29"
"Yo've got that one an' all."
"Why doh yo do yer own card and leave me alone?"
"I cor Ayli, mine's full."

Aynuk: "I'm doing this 'ere quiz. Con yo name an aquatic animal?"
Ayli: "That's a stiff 'un, do yo think it's a ship's cat?"

Cats.
When you have just spread the newspaper a cat will jump on your lap.
The cat sat on the mat...
but only because there was no lap available.
A cat will always ask to leave by the only window or door that is not open.
A cat has no conscience but not every being lacking a conscience has the quality possessed by a cat.

You know you are getting old if you can remember television before snooker was on.

59

Ayli reckons his ancestors day cum over on the Mayflower.

'E says they 'ad a boat of their own and cum straight up Tipton cut.

Aynuk says 'e looked up 'is family tree. 'E says 'e doh know wot wood it was but it was thick.

Soft shoe shuffle

Everyone's got 'designer stubble' these days. It's nothing new. Desperate Dan had it years ago in 'The Dandy.' And they're all wearing trainers. Yet the only exercise some of them get is when they walk from their car into the pub. The only time they run is when " last orders" is called.

So they sit there with the tongue of their trainer half way up their leg licking the outside of their shell suit. They've all got mobile phones because they are the decision makers. Yet they can't decide whether to have another bag of crisps or a packet of nuts!

Ayli: "I'm a bit puzzled by these 'ere mobile phones."

Aynuk: "Ows that our kid?"

Ayli: "Well, if yo doh pay yer bill 'ow dun they cut yer off?"

Aynuk: "Doh ask me mate."

Ayli: "An if yo lost it yo'd 'ave to wait for someone to phone yer afore yo cud find it!"

60

If I don't see you before, have a nice Christmas.

People moan about Christmas. They say it isn't what it used to be. "It's too commercial." Then they dash off to the shops for another pile of cards. You can economise. You can get about 200 in a box for a pound. They're printed on really thin toilet paper and they fall over every time the dog wags his tail but, "It's the thought that counts," isn't it? Presents are a problem. Especially for kids. They seem to get bored with toys really quickly and the batteries are usually flat about two hours after dawn. I think a really good alternative would be to buy them something from the M. F. I. That should keep them occupied until sometime in March.

Supermarkets, at the festive time, always look as though they have been hit by a plague of locusts. People rush up and down the aisles, their arms a blur, like demented mechanical grabs. Rows and rows of trolleys queue at the checkout. You'd think they were a convoy of relief vehicles for the Third World, piled high with nuts, satsumas and turkish delight. Oh! and a selection of orange and lemon sugar coated slices in a round box, because Aunt Hilda likes those. After all it's Christmas, somebody might come! So you wait there at the checkout, stuck behind somebody paying by cheque for one packet of serviettes. And the person behind is poking your backside with a roll of wrapping paper.

Why do we always buy a turkey that is so big you could enter it into the Grand National? You leave it in the kitchen doing pressups and offering the cat outside for a fight. The cat doesn't care. He stands by the oven door rubbing his paws, goading the turkey with cries of, "Cremation!"

One things for sure, you're going to be sick of turkey sandwiches before the new year.

61

The whole Christmas gastronomic experience is really quite strange. Your wife will give you stuffing, cauliflower, sprouts and cabbage followed by rich fruit pudding, satsumas and nuts. Then she tells you off for breaking wind! You've got enough gas to supply the whole of the Blackcountry and you're banished to the garden. As soon as the robins see you coming they board up the bird house windows.

As a nation, we go to excess in every direction. The festive fortnight, to many, is just an excuse for an extended booze up. By Boxing day the empty bottles of liquid pleasure will hang heavily on the minds of a million revellers. They will resurface only to restock for New Years Eve and cry, "Smashing Christmas wasn't it? I can't remember a thing!"

Once again man misses the point completely.

Aynuk says yo con always tell it's Christmas 'cos the binmen start speaking to you!

62

Foreman:
"What would you need to paint that sixty foot chimney?"
Aynuk:
" A sixty foot paint brush!"

Rings a bell?
The new telephone boxes aren't a patch on
the old ones are they?
For a start you can't hear yourself speak.
There's no privacy.
There's no toilet facility
and there's nowhere to put your chip paper.
Bring back the red boxes!

Ayli phoned up the local police station.
"If yo catch the bloke wot broke into my house last night, let me spake to 'im. I want to find out 'ow 'e dun it without wakin' my missus."

Two shopkeepers in the Blackcountry were talking.
"Ows business?" says the first.
"Shockin'" says the other, "Even them as doh pay 'ave
    stopped buying."

63

31st December.
It's almost 10.00pm on the last day of another year.
Already 60,000 people have gathered in Trafalgar
Square.
There is a last minute peace mission in Baghdad
And, as pine needles begin to fall from a million
Christmas trees,
Drunks start to fight in the streets
whilst wishing everyone a happy new year.
Kisses of comfort from the state have been
bestowed on nearly a thousand new year honories
Yet there may be a thousand more worthy who
have been ignored.
Am I becoming more cynical or do my eyes still
twinkle with fresh expectation?
They say that we become more rounded with the
passing of the years.
Tomorrow half the world goes on another diet,
while millions starve, halfbloated with pain.
New Year resolutions may be lost in a broken
January promise
But on the last day of December
good intentions abound and cynics are not
welcome.
Unless, of course, they have a twinkle in their eyes.

64

Little Tommy from Tipton went to the dinner table with very dirty hands. His father sent him away to wash them and told him not to return until they were clean. Several minutes passed and his father called, "Tommy, aren't your hands clean yet?"

"They ay clean yet," Tommy replied, "But I've gorrem to match!"

Every morning since he'd been at the factory, Aynuk had been half an hour late for work. One day, after about six months, he was only five minutes late.

"Well," said the gaffer, "This is the earliest yo've ever bin late fer work."

Ayli says his neighbours are so posh they don't take the dog for a walk, they show him travel brochures.

I'm glad we've got over the Ninja Turtle epidemic. We had proper comic book heroes when I was a kid. Remember Roy of the Rovers?
Now he was a hero. What a great footballer. He made his debut for Melchester Rovers in 1954 and he's still playing today. He must be in his sixties now and he still gets a hat trick every week. I believe the Albion are after him!